ANJITA JAIN

Inspired Laughter

Funny Quotes to Uplift Your Day

Copyright © 2023 by Anjita Jain

All rights reserved. No part of this publication may be reproduced, stored or transmitted in any form or by any means, electronic, mechanical, photocopying, recording, scanning, or otherwise without written permission from the publisher. It is illegal to copy this book, post it to a website, or distribute it by any other means without permission.

This novel is entirely a work of fiction. The names, characters and incidents portrayed in it are the work of the author's imagination. Any resemblance to actual persons, living or dead, events or localities is entirely coincidental.

Anjita Jain asserts the moral right to be identified as the author of this work.

Anjita Jain has no responsibility for the persistence or accuracy of URLs for external or third-party Internet Websites referred to in this publication and does not guarantee that any content on such Websites is, or will remain, accurate or appropriate.

Designations used by companies to distinguish their products are often claimed as trademarks. All brand names and product names used in this book and on its cover are trade names, service marks, trademarks and registered trademarks of their respective owners. The publishers and the book are not associated with any product or vendor mentioned in this book. None of the companies referenced within the book have endorsed the book.

First edition

This book was professionally typeset on Reedsy.
Find out more at reedsy.com

Contents

1

Success, Persistence, Growth and Resilience

“Success is like a lightning bug, it’s brightest when you stop chasing it and just enjoy the glow.”

“They say the sky’s the limit, but we left footprints on the moon.”

“If opportunity doesn’t knock, build a door, or better yet, a whole house. They can’t ignore you then.”

“Failure is not the opposite of success, it’s the stepping stone that says ‘Watch out, genius at work.’”

“Don’t worry about the bumpy road to success; it’s the potholes that keep us awake on the journey.”

“Remember, Rome wasn’t built in a day. But they were laying bricks every hour.”

"Opportunity usually knocks when you're in the shower. Be ready to jump out, just remember to take a towel."

"If you think you've hit rock bottom, remember, even a potato in the dirt can grow into something beautiful."

"Every cloud has a silver lining, but sometimes you need to fly through the storm to see it."

"Keep going, because you didn't come this far to only come this far. And if you did, well, you might want to rethink your travel plans."

"If you're waiting for a sign, this is it. And if it's not, at least you're not waiting anymore."

"Failure is the condiment that gives success its flavor. Without it, success would taste bland."

"Ever tried. Ever failed. No matter. Try again. Fail again. Fail better. And if all else fails, there's always pizza."

"The elevator to success is out of order, but the stairs are always open."

"Perfection is like a unicorn. It's beautiful, magical, and doesn't exist. Be real, not perfect."

"Some see a glass half full, others half empty. Me? I'm grateful I have a glass."

“Opportunities are like sunrises. If you wait too long, you miss them. And no, hitting snooze doesn’t help.”

“Your Monday morning thoughts set the tone for your whole week. So think about coffee and puppies. Lots of puppies.”

“Success is like a bus. Sometimes, you have to run after it. Sometimes, you just have to wait at the stop.”

“Just because you’re trash doesn’t mean you can’t do great things. Remember, it’s called a ‘trash can’, not a ‘trash cannot’.”

“Don’t worry about being a diamond in the rough. Even pearls start as grains of sand.”

“If you don’t like the road you’re walking, pave another one. And if you don’t know how to pave, well, it’s a good time to learn.”

“Sometimes you win, sometimes you learn. And sometimes you just step on a Lego.”

“A diamond is just a piece of charcoal that handled stress exceptionally well. And look at it now, everyone wants it on their finger.”

“Remember, you’re a limited edition. They don’t make ’em like you anymore.”

“Don’t put the key to your happiness in someone else’s pocket. Unless they’re really trustworthy. Or a locksmith.”

"The grass may seem greener on the other side, but maybe that's just because you're not watering your own."

"Remember, even a turtle only makes progress when it sticks its neck out. So, stick your neck out. Metaphorically, of course."

"If at first you don't succeed, redefine success. Or at least take a break with some ice cream."

"You can't control the wind, but you can adjust your sails. And if you're on land, just adjust your hat."

"If you want the rainbow, you have to put up with the rain. Or just use a sprinkler. That works too."

"The road to success is always under construction. Just remember to wear a hard hat."

"The best way to predict the future is to create it. Unless you have a crystal ball. Then definitely use the crystal ball."

"Mistakes are proof that you're trying. And also proof that erasers are a great invention."

"When you reach the end of your rope, tie a knot and hang on. Or make a swing. Swings are fun."

"Remember, Rome wasn't built in a day. But they were laying bricks every hour. So, lay your bricks!"

"If you can't find the key to success, pick the lock. Just kidding, that's illegal. Better yet, build your own door."

"Opportunity doesn't make appointments. You have to be ready when it arrives. And please, wear something nice."

"Great things never came from comfort zones. Except for fuzzy socks. Those are pretty great."

"When you feel like quitting, think about why you started. And if that doesn't work, think about dessert. That usually does the trick."

"Every exit is an entry somewhere else. Just make sure it's not an exit into a shark tank."

"If you want something you've never had, you must be willing to do something you've never done. Like maybe eating broccoli."

"You don't have to be great to start, but you have to start to be great. Or at least to finish that puzzle."

"When one door of happiness closes, another opens. But often we look so long at the closed door that we do not see the one that has been opened. Or we just run into it."

"If you think you are too small to make a difference, try sleeping with a mosquito."

"A river cuts through a rock not because of its power, but because of its persistence. And because it's really, really wet."

“If you don’t like where you are, move. You are not a tree. Unless you’re playing a tree in a play. Then stay put.”

“Remember, it’s okay to be a glowstick. Sometimes we need to break before we can shine.”

“Doubt kills more dreams than failure ever will. So, shoot for the moon. Even if you miss, you’ll... probably get lost in space. So, actually, just aim carefully.”

“The best way to predict your future is to create it. Unless you have a time machine. Then you’re set.”

“Every accomplishment starts with the decision to try. And every cake starts with the decision to bake.”

“Even if you’re on the right track, you’ll get run over if you just sit there. So, move! Or at least get a comfy chair.”

“Hardships often prepare ordinary people for an extraordinary destiny. Or at least a really good memoir.”

“Believe you can and you’re halfway there. Believe you can’t and you’re probably right. So, think positive!”

“Behind every successful person is a substantial amount of coffee. And an alarm clock. Definitely an alarm clock.”

“Success is not the key to happiness. Happiness is the key to success. The key to the front door, however, is still pretty important.”

"You can't make an omelet without breaking eggs. But you can make a mess without doing anything at all. Aim for the omelet."

"Every sunrise is an invitation to brighten someone's day. Or at least to stop hitting the snooze button."

"People often say motivation doesn't last. Well, neither does bathing. That's why it's recommended daily. Same goes for eating chocolate."

"The question isn't who is going to let me; it's who is going to stop me. Unless it's about eating the last slice of pizza, then it's definitely about who's going to let me."

"Believe in yourself so strongly that the world can't help but believe in you too. Like how strongly we believe in coffee."

"You are never too old to set another goal or to dream a new dream. Or to have cereal for dinner."

"You only fail when you stop trying. Or when you run out of tries. In that case, you might need to buy some more."

"Every wall is a door if you believe in yourself. And own a sledgehammer."

"A smooth sea never made a skilled sailor. But it does make for a great beach day."

"Don't wait for the opportunity. Create it. Just like you create that perfect sandwich."

"The road to success is dotted with many tempting parking spaces. Remember, that's how they get you."

"Your future self is watching you right now through memories. So, be cool. No pressure."

"If you don't know where you want to go, then it doesn't matter which path you take. As long as it leads to pizza."

"Success is not the key to happiness. But it can open a lot of doors."

"Remember, a diamond is a chunk of coal that did well under pressure. So, don't feel bad about your stress level, you're just carbon and pressure away from being a gem."

"Success is often the result of taking a misstep in the right direction. Like mistakenly going into the wrong room and finding the surprise party they've planned for you."

"If you hit the target every time, it's too near or too big. So, move it further, make it smaller, or get a bigger dart."

"Your life does not get better by chance, it gets better by change. And by adding more puppies."

"The best way to predict the future is to create it. Or invest in a really good crystal ball."

"The best way to predict your future is to create it. And to keep a good calendar."

"The only thing standing between you and your goal is the ridiculous story you keep telling yourself as to why you can't achieve it. And maybe that giant pile of laundry."

2

Add Your Own Inspired Laughter Moments

1.

2.

3.

4.

5.

6.

7.

8.

9.

3

Humor, Witticism, Reality and Perspective

"When life gives you lemons, make orange juice and leave the world wondering how you did it."

"Procrastination is my favorite hobby, I'll tell you why... tomorrow."

"You don't have to be crazy to achieve greatness – but honestly, it does help to have a screw loose."

"When life shuts a door, open it again. It's a door, that's how they work."

"They say you can't have your cake and eat it too. But what's the point of a cake if you can't eat it?"

"Being an adult is mostly googling how to do stuff while trying not to look like you're googling how to do stuff."

"To those who say money can't buy happiness: ever tried buying a tub of your favorite ice cream?"

"Strive for progress, not perfection. Unless you're making a soufflé. In that case, perfection is pretty important."

"Remember, the early bird gets the worm. But the second mouse gets the cheese."

"People say money doesn't grow on trees, but remember that paper comes from trees. Coincidence? I think not!"

"The road to success is dotted with tempting parking spaces. Don't park, keep driving."

"Even when you're on the right track, you'll get run over if you just sit there. So, get moving!"

"If you think your boss is tough, wait till you get a cat. They don't negotiate."

"Some people are like clouds. When they disappear, it's a brighter day."

"Change is inevitable, except from a vending machine."

"They say the grass is greener on the other side, but remember, it's also just as hard to mow."

"An apple a day keeps anyone away if thrown hard enough. But remember, kindness is a better solution."

"People say nothing is impossible, but I do nothing every day. So technically, I'm doing the impossible daily."

"When life closes a door, just open it again. It's a door. That's how it works."

"If people are trying to bring you down, it only means that you are above them."

"It's easy to stand with the crowd. It takes courage to stand alone. Especially when there's pizza."

"If you can't find the sunshine, be the sunshine. If you can't be the sunshine, get a sunlamp."

"When nothing goes right, go left. Unless you're on a one-way street. Then, you should probably follow the law."

"The quickest way to double your money is to fold it in half and put it back in your pocket. Or buy two chocolate bars for the price of one."

"You can't have everything. Where would you put it? Unless you have a really big house, then maybe."

"Hard work never killed anyone, but why take the chance? Just kidding, roll up those sleeves!"

"To the world you may be one person, but to one person you may be the world. Or their favorite pizza delivery person."

"An optimist believes that we live in the best of all possible worlds. A pessimist fears this is true. A realist just orders pizza."

"If you're feeling down, remember: the view from the top wouldn't be as spectacular without the climb."

"If your dreams don't scare you, they're not big enough. Or maybe you just dream about puppies. In that case, carry on."

"They say don't burn your bridges, but sometimes that's the only way to stop the zombies from following you."

"Never let your fear decide your future. Unless you're a fortune teller, then maybe reconsider."

"The only time you should ever look back is to see how far you've come. Or to make sure you didn't leave the stove on."

"People often say that motivation doesn't last. Well, neither does bathing - that's why we recommend it daily."

"Never look down on anybody unless you're helping them up. Or you're really tall. Then it might be unavoidable."

"Remember, you're unique. Just like everyone else."

"Life is a journey, and if you fall in love with the journey, you will be in love forever. If you fall in love with a pizza, that's okay too."

"They say that love is more important than money, but have you ever tried to pay your bills with a hug?"

"If you stumble, make it part of the dance. Unless you're carrying a tray of drinks. Then just try not to stumble."

"Don't give up on your dreams. Keep sleeping."

"Sometimes the wrong choices bring us to the right places. Like that one time you took a wrong turn and found the best ice cream shop."

"Happiness is an inside job. Unfortunately, it doesn't come with a manual. Or a tool belt."

"Sometimes the best thing you can do is not think, not wonder, not imagine, not obsess. Just breathe and have faith. And maybe eat a cookie."

"Life isn't about waiting for the storm to pass, it's about learning to dance in the rain. Or at least getting a really good umbrella."

"Your value doesn't decrease based on someone's inability to see your worth. Unless they're an appraiser. Then you might have a problem."

"Don't judge each day by the harvest you reap, but by the seeds that you plant. And remember, chocolate doesn't grow on trees."

"Just remember, every day may not be good, but there's something good in every day. Like that first cup of coffee."

"Sometimes when you're in a dark place you think you've been buried, but you've actually been planted. Like a carrot. But with more existential dread."

"If you're too open-minded, your brains will fall out. So keep a healthy skepticism, but don't lose your sense of wonder."

"Age is of no importance unless you're a cheese. Or a fine wine."

"Don't wait for the perfect moment, take the moment and make it perfect. Or take a nap. Naps are good too."

"An apple a day keeps anyone away if you throw it hard enough. But, remember, it's better to share than to throw."

"They say money can't buy happiness. But it can buy chocolate, which is kind of the same thing."

"Always be yourself. Unless you can be a unicorn. Then, always be a unicorn."

"Never let anyone treat you like regular glue. You are glitter glue."

"Be the kind of person your dog thinks you are. Unless your dog thinks you're a squirrel. Then maybe reconsider."

"When life gives you lemons, make orange juice and leave the world wondering how you did it."

"The best view comes after the hardest climb. Or a scenic

elevator ride."

"A journey of a thousand miles begins with a single step. And a really good pair of sneakers."

"If you can't convince them, confuse them. Unless you're trying to give directions. In that case, please don't."

"If you can't get rid of the skeleton in your closet, you'd best teach it to dance. Or at least to dust your shelves."

"Imagination is more important than knowledge. Knowledge is limited, imagination encircles the world. And also creates unicorns."

"When life gives you a rainy day, play in the puddles. But remember to wear your rain boots."

"A day without sunshine is like, you know, night. And a night without stars is like, you know, cloudy."

"Don't wait for your ship to come in, swim out to it. Unless you're scared of water. Then maybe just rent a speedboat."

"Sometimes you win, sometimes you learn. And sometimes you just step in something sticky."

"In the middle of every difficulty lies opportunity. And sometimes a really good sandwich."

"No one can make you feel inferior without your consent. Except maybe a really talented mime."

"Believe you can and you're halfway there. Unless 'there' is very far away. Then you might still have a bit of a journey."

"You're never too old to do goofy stuff. Remember, age is a high price to pay for maturity."

"Sometimes the wrong choices bring us to the right places. Like that time you took a wrong turn and discovered a new coffee shop."

"Laugh at your problems, everyone else does. And if they don't, they probably haven't heard the joke yet."

"When nothing goes right, go left. Unless you're on a one-way street. That might cause issues."

"Never follow someone else's path unless you're in the woods and you're lost and you see a path. By all means, you should follow that."

"Opportunity does not knock, it presents itself when you beat down the door. Or when you accidentally stumble upon it while looking for the bathroom."

4

Add Your Own Inspired Laughter Moments

1.
2.
3.
4.
5.
6.
7.
8.
9.

5

Life, Perseverance, Dreams, Action and Aspirations

"Life is like a bicycle. Just when you think you're cruising, you hit a pothole. The trick is to keep pedaling."

"Always remember you're unique, just like everyone else."

"If you ever feel like you're on the wrong path, remember that wrong turns make the best stories."

"Chase your dreams like a dog chases its tail, with relentless joy and a bit of silliness."

"If you think you're too small to make a difference, try sleeping with a mosquito in the room."

"Don't take life too seriously, no one gets out alive anyway."

"Don't chase happiness. Be like a sunflower, stand tall and let happiness chase you."

"If life is like a box of chocolates, remember, you're the one holding the box."

"Don't wait for your ship to come in, swim out to it. But do remember to wear a life jacket."

"Life's a garden; dig it, plant it, weed it. And if it all fails, make a mud pie."

"When life throws tomatoes at you, make a salsa. Dance to the rhythm of life."

"When life gives you a rainy day, play in the puddles. Or better yet, start a puddle-jumping contest."

"Life is like a cup of tea, it's all in how you brew it. And if it's still bitter, try adding some sugar."

"If you feel like you're losing everything, remember that trees lose their leaves every year and they still stand tall and wait for better days to come."

"Dreams are like soap bubbles. They may pop, but that shouldn't stop you from blowing more."

"People say 'reach for the stars', but they forget to mention the space suit. Be prepared!"

"Success is like a game of chess. You don't win by just moving forward; sometimes, you have to move sideways or even take a step back."

"Life is like a roller coaster. It has its ups and downs, but it's your choice to scream or enjoy the ride."

"Behind every great person is a great coffee machine. Brew your success, one cup at a time."

"If plan A fails, remember you have 25 more letters left. If you're bilingual, even better."

"When you feel like quitting, think about why you started. If that doesn't work, think about puppies. Works every time."

"Life is like a camera. Focus on what's important, capture the good times, and if things don't work out, just take another shot."

"You are never too old to set another goal or dream a new dream. Or eat a new flavor of ice cream."

"Life is like a bicycle. To keep your balance, you must keep moving. Also, don't forget to ring the bell now and then."

"Life is like a book. Some chapters are sad, some are happy, and some are just really confusing."

"When life gives you a hundred reasons to break down and cry, show life that you have a million reasons to smile and laugh."

"Remember, every exit is an entrance to somewhere else. Unless it's a one-way street. Then it's just an exit."

"Some days you're the pigeon, some days you're the statue. Just remember to pack an umbrella."

"If life gives you lemons, make lemonade. But if life gives you limes, a margarita may be a better option."

"Remember, life is like riding a bicycle. To keep your balance, you must keep moving. And wear a helmet. Safety first."

"The grass is greener where you water it. Unless you paint it. But that's considered cheating."

"Where there's a will, there's a way. And where there's a way, there's usually a GPS."

"Every cloud has a silver lining. But not every muffin has a chocolate center. Remember to check before you bite."

"Your mind is like this water, my friend, when it is agitated it becomes difficult to see. But when you allow it to settle, the answer becomes clear. Also, don't drink it. It's metaphorical water."

"The key to success is to start before you're ready. The key to a good cake, however, is to make sure the oven is preheated."

"Life is like a sandwich, no matter which way you flip it, the bread always comes first. And so does a good attitude."

"The best time to plant a tree was 20 years ago. The second-best time is now. Unless it's night. Then you should probably wait until morning."

"Live each day like it's your last. But pay your bills and do your laundry just in case it isn't."

"Life isn't about finding yourself. It's about finding the remote control."

"Life is short. Smile while you still have teeth. Or while you still have spinach in them."

"In the book of life, the answers aren't in the back. They're usually in the footnotes or hidden somewhere in chapter three."

"You are what you eat, so stay sweet. And occasionally indulge in some cheesecake."

"Kindness is free, sprinkle that stuff everywhere. Just like confetti. But less messy."

"Do not take life too seriously. You will never get out of it alive. Also, you'll ruin the party."

"Life is like a camera. Just focus on what's important, capture the good times, develop from the negatives, and if things don't work out, just take another shot. And remember to delete the embarrassing ones."

"The best way to succeed in life is to act on the advice you give to others. Unless you're advising someone on how to beat you at Monopoly."

"The only place where your dreams become impossible is in your own thinking. Unless you dream of becoming a mermaid. Then it might be a bit tricky."

"We are all a little broken. But the last time I checked, broken crayons still color."

"The bad news is time flies. The good news is you're the pilot. The bad news again is that you need to learn how to fly."

"Sometimes life is about risking everything for a dream no one can see but you. And sometimes it's just about trying a new flavor of ice cream."

"Do not let what you cannot do interfere with what you can do. Unless what you cannot do is stop eating cookies. Then you should probably address that first."

"Life is like a bicycle. To keep your balance, you must keep moving. But remember to stop and refuel at ice cream shops."

"If you're going through hell, keep going. And remember to take a water break, it's quite hot down there."

"If you think you're too small to make a difference, try sleeping in a room with a mosquito."

"The elevator to success is out of order. You'll have to use the stairs, one step at a time. And remember, there's no escalator either."

"If you think you can, you can. And if you think you can't, try anyway. Then order pizza. You've earned it."

"Life is like a game of cards. The hand you are dealt is determinism; the way you play it is free will. And sometimes you just need to reshuffle."

6

Add Your Own Inspired Laughter Moments

1.

2.

3.

4.

5.

6.

7.

8.

9.

7

About the Author

Anjita (Anji) Jain is a humor enthusiast, a collector of quotes, and a believer in the power of laughter. With 'Inspired Laughter', she hopes to spread joy, uplift spirits, and remind everyone that life is better when you're laughing.

www.ingramcontent.com/pod-product-compliance
Lightning Source LLC
La Vergne TN
LVHW090541110826
845146LV00003B/1223

* 9 7 9 8 9 8 8 7 3 4 4 2 0 *